MW00884687

God's Creation Story Coloring Book

Bible Learning for Toddlers and Kids

The Creation Story is simplified
for toddlers and kids, adapted from the Holy Bible.
Copyright © 2024 LambLibrary Press. All rights reserved. First Edition.

This publication may not be reproduced in whole or in part by
any means without permission from the copyright owners.
Permission is never granted for commercial purposes.

 LambLibrary Press

Dear friend,

You know, the world is more complicated than we see.

For example, water, steam, and ice are made of atoms. We don't see them, but they are there.

Similarly, we cannot see the solar system without a telescope, but it is also there.

Have you ever wondered who created this complex world of atoms, planets, our Earth, everything on Earth, and everything in space?

We call Him God, the Creator of all things on Earth and in the skies.

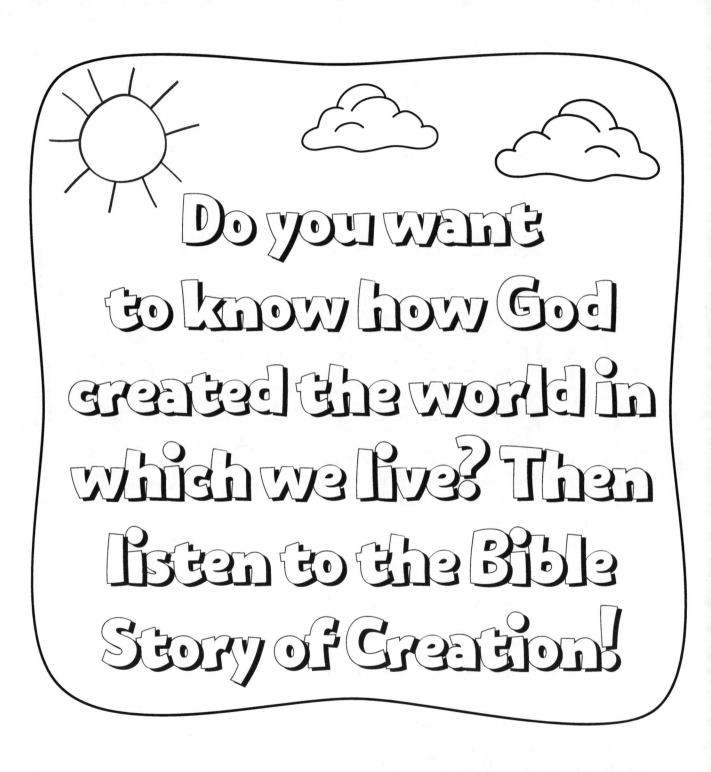

Do you want to know how God created the world in which we live? Then listen to the Bible Story of Creation!

Day 1

Genesis 1:1-5

In the beginning, there was nothing but darkness. Then, God said, "Let there be LIGHT," and there was light. And God called the light "day" and the darkness "night." This was the first day.

In the beginning, there was nothing but darkness.

Cover your eyes with your palms, and imagine how dark it was!

Day 2

Genesis 1:6-8

On the second day, God created the SKY above and the WATER below.

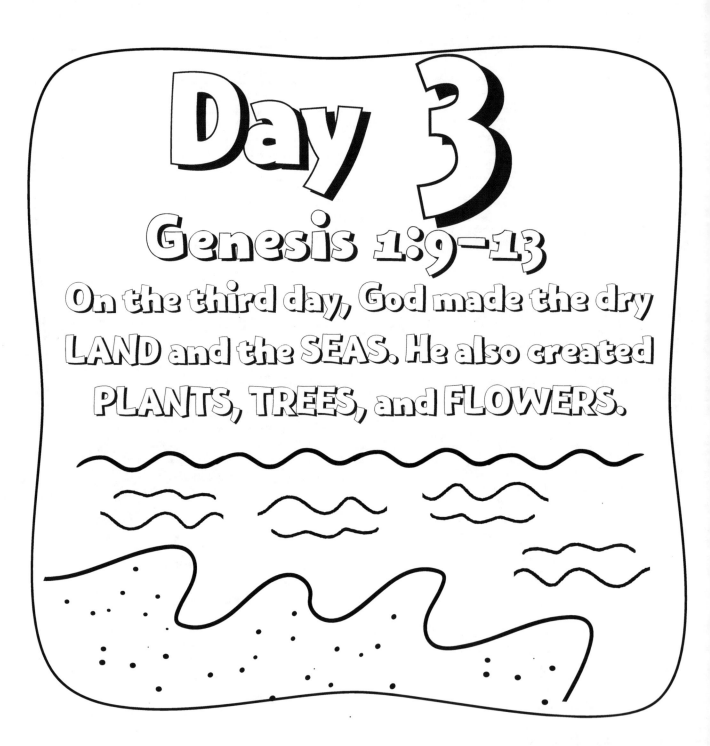

God created various PLANTS, GRASS, TREES, FLOWERS on the third day.

Day 4

Genesis 1:14-19

On the fourth day, God created the SUN to rule the day and the MOON to rule the night. He also made the STARS.

MOON

SUN

STARS

God created the SUN to rule the DAY.
God created the MOON to rule the NIGHT.

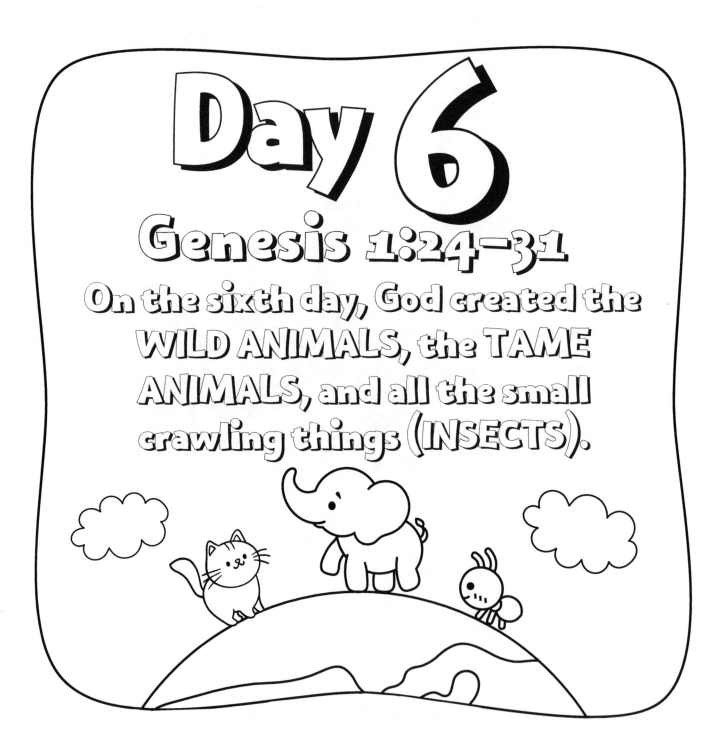

WILD ANIMALS

TAME ANIMALS

INSECTS

Then, God created the first MAN, Adam, and the first WOMAN, Eve.

God created the WILD ANIMALS

God created the
INSECTS

Day 7

Genesis 2:1-3

So the earth, the sky, and everything in them were finished. So on the seventh day, GOD RESTED from His work.

On the seventh day, God rested from all the work he did while creating the world.

GOD'S REST

And do you know what happened next?

God placed Adam and Eve
in a beautiful garden called Eden.

He allowed them to eat from any tree
in the garden except for one—the tree
of the knowledge of good and evil.

Adam and Eve lived happily in the
garden until one day, a crafty serpent
tempted Eve to eat fruit from the
forbidden tree.

But even though Adam and Eve disobeyed God, He still loved them. He promised to send a Savior who would one day make things right again.

And that's how God created the world and the first humans, Adam and Eve.

God is the creator of the world.
Here are some questions to
review your knowledge:

1) On what day did God create light? (First day)

2) On what day did God create the sky and water? (Second day)

3) On what day did God create the land, seas, and plants? (Third day)

God is the creator of the world. Here are some questions to review your knowledge:

4) On what day did God create the sun, moon, and stars? (Fourth day)

5) On what day did God create fish and birds? (Fifth day)

6) On what day did God create animals, insects, and humans? (Sixth day)

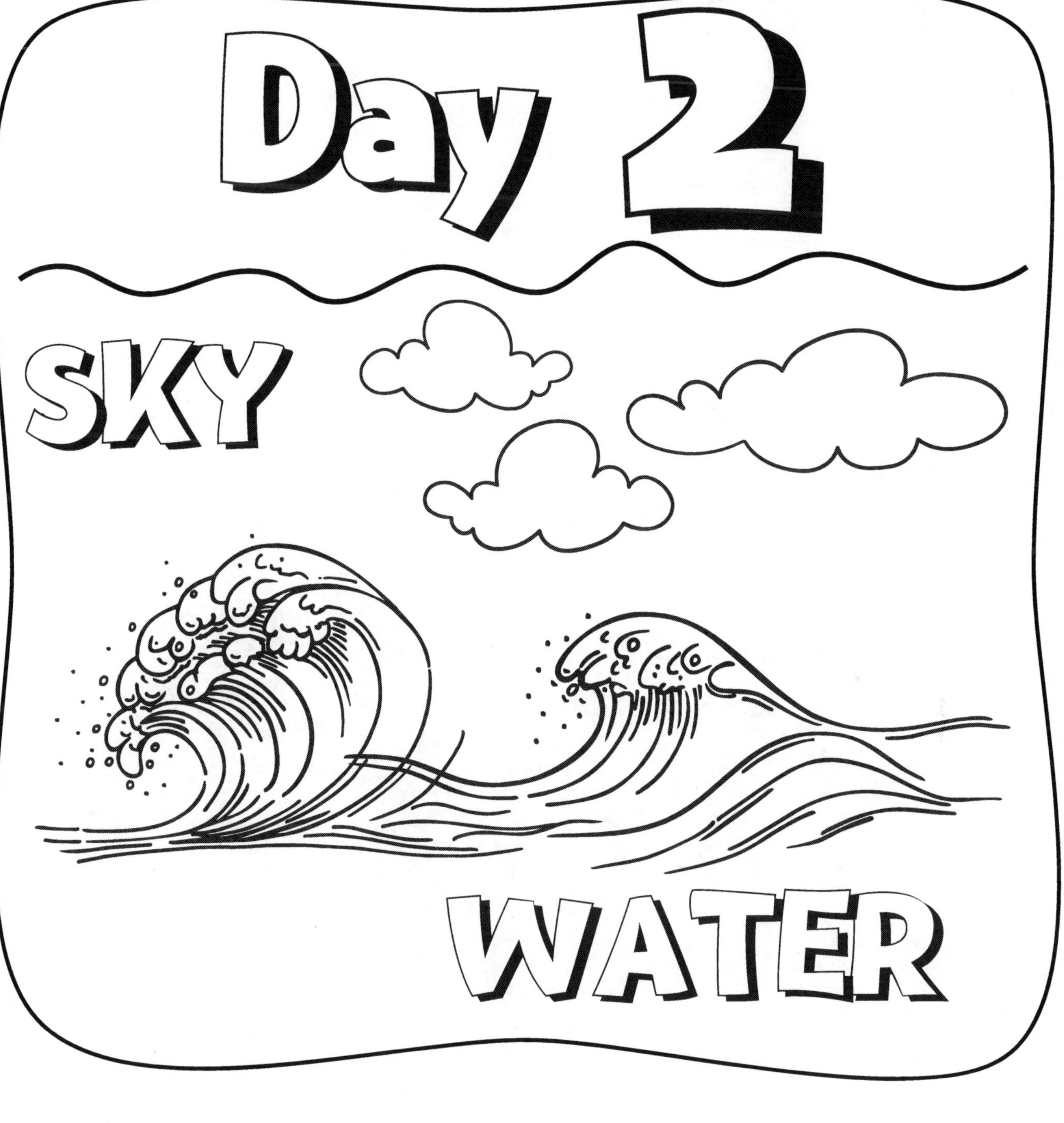
Day 2
SKY
WATER

Day 5

BIRDS in the SKY

FISH in the SEAS

Day 6

ANIMALS

INSECTS

HUMANS

Creative Task

God created us in His own image, which means being creative and having a great imagination. He created many different plants, birds, fish, animals, and insects. If this were your task, what kind of animal, plant, insect, fish, and bird would you create? What colors and shapes would they have? Imagine and draw! Don't forget to come up with names for them too!

Imagine and draw the PLANT! Come up with a name!

_____

- -

_____

Imagine and draw the BIRD!
Come up with a name!

_____

- -

_____

Imagine and draw the FISH!
Come up with a name!

_____

- -

_____

Imagine and draw the ANIMAL!
Come up with a name!

_____

- -

_____

Imagine and draw the INSECT!
Come up with a name!

_____

- -

_____

Great job! You are so talented and creative!

Do you know that God loves you, saves you, and helps you every day?

EVERY DAY
GOD THINKS OF YOU!
(Jeremiah 29:11)

EVERY MINUTE
GOD CARES FOR YOU!
(1 Peter 5:7)

BECAUSE EVERY SECOND
HE LOVES YOU!
(1 John 4:16)

Thank you for reading!

If you can spare a few minutes to leave us a review, we'd be super grateful!

LambLibrary Press Team

Copyright © 2024 LambLibrary Press. All rights reserved. First Edition.

 LambLibrary Press

Made in the USA
Columbia, SC
10 August 2024

40303096R00059